Nellie Bly's

Daring Trip Around the World

written by **Agnieszka Biskup**

illustrated by **Natalia Galindo**

CAPSTONE PRESS
a capstone imprint

Published by Capstone Press, an imprint of Capstone
1710 Roe Crest Drive, North Mankato, Minnesota 56003
capstonepub.com

Library of Congress Cataloging-in-Publication Data is available on the Library of Congress website.

ISBN: 9781669017059 (hardcover)
ISBN: 9781669017004 (paperback)
ISBN: 9781669017011 (ebook PDF)

Summary: On November 14, 1889, newspaper reporter Nellie Bly set out on the trip of a lifetime. Equipped with just one small bag of necessities, she planned to circle the globe in a mere 75 days. In a time of steamships, locomotives, and horse-drawn carriages, few thought she could do it. But bravery and determination carried her through. How did Bly complete her historic journey, and what is its enduring legacy?

Editorial Credits
Editor: Christopher Harbo; Designer: Tracy Davies; Production Specialist: Katy LaVigne

Design Element by Shutterstock/kzww

All internet sites appearing in back matter were available and accurate when this book was sent to press.

Direct quotations appear in bold italicized text on the following pages:
Pages 8–10, 14–17, 21, 23, 25, 27, from *Around the World in Seventy-Two Days* by Nellie Bly (Mint Editions, 2021).

Printed and bound in China 5379

TABLE OF CONTENTS

Introduction Dreams of World Travel

Famous American reporter Nellie Bly wasn't always known as Nellie Bly. She was born Elizabeth Jane Cochran in 1864.

Bly was a child when Jules Verne's book *Around the World in Eighty Days* was published in 1873. That novel, describing how the fictional Phileas Fogg traveled the globe in 80 days, was a worldwide bestseller.

This Frenchman's book is pure fantasy! It would take at least a year to travel around the world––maybe even longer.

What if your ship sank? Or you got sick from a tropical fever?

But it's such a romantic story!

And it was true. No one then thought a trip like Fogg's was possible. After all, there were no planes or computers. Trains, boats, and horse-drawn wagons were the main means of transportation.

Traveling was also dangerous. Storms, fires, icebergs, train derailments, bandits, and disease could turn a trip deadly.

But a few things happened in the 1800s that made a trip like Fogg's more possible. In 1869, the first transcontinental railroad was finished in the United States. Horse-drawn wagons and stagecoaches were no longer the only way to cross the country.

That same year, the Suez Canal opened in the Middle East. Now ships could easily sail between Europe and Asia instead of traveling around the African continent.

Young Elizabeth had no idea that she would be the first person to travel around the world in 80 days. In fact, she'd do it even faster!

Chapter 1 An Unexpected Career

Sadly, Elizabeth's father died when she was six. Her mother remarried, hoping her new husband would take care of her and her children. But Nellie's stepfather was violent. Her mother got a divorce, which was very uncommon at the time.

What will I do?

As a teenager, Elizabeth resolved that she would never rely on a man to take care of her.

I need to work! But I can't find any jobs that pay a decent wage.

SEAMSTRESS NEEDED

NANNY WANTED

HOUSEKEEPER WANTED

Then she read an article in her local newspaper, the *Pittsburgh Dispatch*. It changed her life.

Mother, have you seen this horrible article? The author says women should only cook, clean, sew, and take care of children.

He says women who work outside the home are "a monstrosity!"

Elizabeth was furious. She wrote a letter to the newspaper's editor.

Women have to work to support themselves too. They are just as capable as men. They should have careers if they want them.

The editor was so impressed with her letter that he hired her as a writer for his paper.

But women can't write under their real names. It's just not proper. We need something neat and catchy.

You already have a Bessie Bramble.

Hmm. There's that popular song right now called "Nelly Bly." How about writing under that name?

Thanks to a spelling mistake, Elizabeth became Nellie Bly instead.

The paper, however, didn't give Nellie enough serious news stories to write. So in 1887, after two years with the *Dispatch*, she wrote a short note . . .

I AM OFF FOR NEW YORK. LOOK OUT FOR ME. BLY

. . . and left Pittsburgh to look for a better job.

DISPATCH

DAILY DISPATCH OFFICE

Nellie was eventually hired by the *New York World* newspaper. To get the job, she agreed to pose as a mentally ill patient at the Women's Asylum on Blackwell's Island. Her stories about the terrible conditions she uncovered made her famous.

Nellie worked very hard. Her exciting and daring undercover stories helped the *World* sell more papers. And she was making enough money to bring her mother to live with her in New York.

So what story will you write next?

I don't know. I've been working so hard. And I still need to come up with some new story ideas for my editor tomorrow.

I can't sleep.

I wish I was at the other end of the earth!

I need a vacation; why not take a trip around the world? If I could do it as quickly as Phileas Fogg did, I should go.

Nellie had her idea.

The next day she studied dozens of steamship timetables. She thought she could travel the world in 80 days, but would the *World* agree? She spoke to her editor.

Have you any ideas?

I want to go around the world in eighty days or less. I think I can beat Phileas Fogg's record. May I try it?

Hmm . . . Let me check with our business manager.

To her dismay, she found the paper already had the idea, but wanted to send a man.

It's impossible! You are a woman and need a protector. Even if you did travel alone, all your luggage would slow you down.

There is no use talking about it; no one but a man can do this.

Very well. Start the man, and I'll start the same day for some other newspaper and beat him.

I believe you would.

The paper eventually promised that if they did decide to do the story, Nellie would be the reporter to go.

9

About one year later, on a cold, wet November evening in 1889, Nellie received a message from her editor.

What did I do this time?

Come to the office at once!

Can you start around the world [the] day after tomorrow?

I can start this minute.

The *World* editors wanted Nellie to leave on a steamship bound for England Thursday morning. Nellie agreed. But she had to get a few supplies first.

The next morning, Nellie went to a dressmaker to order a dress for her journey.

I need a dress that can stand constant wear for three months and I need it by this evening.

It usually takes a few days to make a dress.

Nonsense! If you want to do it, you can do it. The question is, do you want to do it?

Let me get some materials. This blue broadcloth should do nicely.

Nellie bought a coat and a cap for her trip. She also chose a leather bag about the size of a small backpack.

After picking up her new clothes, Nellie focused on packing everything into her tiny bag.

With one bag, I can concentrate on traveling, making my connections, and not worry about luggage.

Oof! I didn't realize packing a small bag would be so hard!

Now I just have to go to the newspaper office to pick up travel money and my passport.

Nellie was finally ready to start her journey in the morning. If nothing went wrong, she thought it should take 75 days to circle the globe.

Chapter 2 Going Around the World

Nellie and her editors had her trip planned out in advance. They decided she would go eastward around the world. Nellie knew all the connections she would make by boat and train.

START/FINISH

Nellie's Plan

Steamship: Hoboken, New Jersey, to Southampton, England.

Train: Southampton to London; London to Folkestone.

Ferry: Folkestone to Boulogne, France.

Train: Boulogne to Amiens; Amiens to Brindisi, Italy.

Steamship: Brindisi to Port Said, Egypt; Port Said to Aden (in modern Yemen); Aden to Colombo, Ceylon (now called Sri Lanka); Colombo to Penang (in modern Malaysia); Penang to Singapore; Singapore to Hong Kong; Hong Kong to Yokohama, Japan; Yokohama to San Francisco, California.

Train: San Francisco to Mojave, California; Mojave to Albuquerque, New Mexico; Albuquerque to La Junta, Colorado; La Junta to Chicago, Illinois; Chicago to Columbus, Ohio; Columbus to Philadelphia, Pennsylvania; Philadelphia to Jersey City, New Jersey.

On November 14, 1889, at 9:40 a.m., Nellie set sail from Hoboken, New Jersey. The *World* put the story on their front page that same day. Nellie traveled on the luxurious ocean liner SS *Augusta Victoria*, destined for England.

This ship recently broke the record for the fastest westbound crossing of the Atlantic.

I know. It reached New York in seven days. The speed is unbelievable!

It's only a matter of 28,000 miles, and seventy-five days and four hours, until I should be back again.

Nellie had never taken a sea voyage before.

So you've started on your big trip? Do you get seasick?

And she's going around the world!

Nellie was traveling on a first-class ticket and was invited to eat at the captain's table.

The only way to conquer seasickness is by forcing one's self to eat.

Nellie left the table three times because she was sick. Finally, exhausted, she went to her cabin and to bed.

The next day, Nellie woke to a voice at her cabin's door.

We were afraid that you were dead.

I always sleep late in the morning.

It is half-past four in the evening!

But the sleep did Nellie good. Her seasickness went away.

The weather was bad and the seas were rough, but she enjoyed her voyage.

On November 21, land was finally sighted. Nellie had reached England.

At 2:00 a.m. on November 22, a tugboat carried Nellie to the wharf at Southampton. Tracy Greaves, the London reporter for the *World*, met her with some exciting news.

Mr. and Mrs. Jules Verne have sent a special letter asking if you could visit them.

Oh, I'd love to, but I don't think I have enough time.

If you are willing to go without sleep and rest for two nights, I think it can be done.

Nellie and Greaves took a mail train from Southampton and arrived in London early that morning. Then they took a horse-drawn cab.

There's the River Thames and there's Westminster Abbey . . .

In this fog, all I can see is a blur.

Nellie didn't have much time for sightseeing anyway. She had to get a special passport, pick up her messages at the *World*'s London offices, and buy tickets for part of her journey.

Now Nellie hurried to meet Jules Verne, the man who had inspired her adventure, in Amiens, France.

Don't forget! You still have another ferry and train to catch to Amiens!

Verne met Nellie at the train platform, along with his wife, and a journalist who would be Nellie's translator. The Vernes did not speak English, and Nellie did not speak French.

《It is really not to be believed that this little girl is going all alone around the world. She looks like a mere child.》

《She is trim, energetic, and strong. I believe, Jules, that she will make your heroes look foolish; she will beat your record.》

At his large home, Verne showed Nellie the tiny study where he wrote his famous novels and his map of Fogg's journey. He even drew Nellie's route on it.

《If you do it in seventy-nine days, I shall applaud with both hands.》

Meeting Verne slowed Nellie down a bit, but it got everyone talking. She made the front page of the *World*, and other newspapers began following her story too.

Extra! Extra! Nellie Bly meets Jules Verne!

To keep readers interested, the *World* ran a contest. Whoever could guess Nellie's arrival time would win a free trip to Europe. Almost a million entries poured in during her journey.

THE NELLIE BLY GUESSING MATCH

Chapter 3 Forward from France

After visiting the Vernes, Nellie took a train to Brindisi, Italy.

Fog and cold again! I can't see a thing. I thought Italy was supposed to be sunny.

It's better than being attacked by bandits. They robbed this train last week.

At least that would have been exciting.

Nellie arrived in Brindisi at 1:30 a.m. on November 25, a few hours later than expected. From Brindisi, she was to set sail for Egypt.

Do I have time to go to the telegraph office before my ship leaves? I'd like to send a message.

If you hurry. Let me show you the way.

I'd like to send a message to the *World* newspaper in New York that I've arrived in Brindisi.

That is fine. But where exactly is New York?

It took some time explaining, but the message was finally sent.

Then they heard a ship's whistle.

WHOOT! WHOOT!

Oh, no! Is my ship leaving without me?

Can you run?

Luckily, the whistle had come from another departing ship. Nellie's ship, the *Victoria*, was still there.

Nellie's voyage on the *Victoria* across the Mediterranean Sea was tiresome. A rumor that she was an American heiress traveling with a hairbrush and a bankbook got her some unwelcome attention from fortune hunters.

I'm the second son of an earl. I'm looking for a wife who will help me pay my bills. Would you marry me?

No.

Occasionally, the *Victoria* dropped anchor and Nellie would go ashore. In Port Said, Egypt, she bought a hat to protect her from the sun.

The next morning, Nellie got up early so she could see the famous Suez Canal.

They started building the canal in 1859. It took ten years.

It looks like we're sailing through an enormous ditch. But at least it's making my trip around the world possible.

From Egypt, Nellie traveled to the town of Aden, in modern-day Yemen. She and some other passengers went ashore.

So you use these small sticks of wood to polish your teeth? They're much better than the tooth-destroying brushes used in America.

On December 8, the *Victoria* reached Colombo, Ceylon (now Sri Lanka), two days ahead of schedule. Nellie used her extra time to see the sights and ride in a rickshaw for the first time.

Nellie planned to take a ship named the *Oriental* to Hong Kong. But there was a delay. The *Oriental* couldn't leave until another ship called the *Nepaul* came in. All Nellie could think of was her deadline.

When will we sail?

As soon as the *Nepaul* comes in. She was to have been here at daybreak. She's a slow old boat.

May she go to the bottom of the bay when she does get in. The old tub!

Wait! There's the *Nepaul!* At last!

But Nellie was now behind schedule.

Thanks to the *Nepaul*, the *Oriental* left port three days later than expected. The ship stopped briefly at Penang and Singapore. Though Nellie didn't make many purchases in Penang, she saw a macaque monkey in Singapore she had to buy.

I'm going to call you McGinty.

It traveled with her for the rest of her journey.

On the way to Hong Kong, the *Oriental* encountered massive storms, but it still arrived two days ahead of schedule on December 23. It broke all records for the fastest passage from Colombo to Hong Kong.

Once in Hong Kong, Nellie made her way to the steamship company's office.

I need the earliest ship sailing to Japan.

What is your name?

Nellie Bly.

Oh, you're going to be beaten.

I think not. I've made up my delay.

You are going to lose it.

Lose it? I don't understand.

Aren't you having a race around the world?

Yes, I'm running a race with time.

Time? No, that's not her name. You're racing Elizabeth Bisland. She left Hong Kong three days ago and is going to win.

And that's how Nellie found out she was racing against another woman traveling around the world. Sponsored by *Cosmopolitan* magazine, Bisland had left New York on the same day Nellie left New Jersey. But Bisland was traveling west instead of east.

Nellie was surprised but decided it didn't matter.

I promised my editor that I would go around the world in seventy-five days, and if I accomplish that I shall be satisfied. I am not racing with anyone.

If someone else wants to do the trip in less time, that is their concern.

To add to her worries, Nellie had to wait five days for her next boat, the *Oceanic*. As she waited, she explored Hong Kong, visiting shops and temples.

At last, the *Oceanic* was ready to sail on December 28. But Nellie soon learned that McGinty's transfer to the new ship was not without incident.

Is my monkey all right? What happened to your arm? What did you do?

I didn't do anything. It was the monkey that did this to me. All I did was scream!

Nellie celebrated New Year's Eve with the other passengers aboard the *Oceanic*.

Happy 1890!

Before Nellie knew it, she was in Japan. With a few days free, she went sightseeing.

Japan is so beautiful!

But I still look forward to getting home.

On January 7, 1890, Nellie left Yokohama, Japan, on her final sea voyage to San Francisco, California. The *Oceanic*'s chief engineer showed Nellie the poem his men had written for her in the engine room.

for Nellie Bly, We'll win or die
January 20, 1890

The whole crew is cheering you on, Nellie Bly! We'll do our best to get you to San Francisco on the twentieth!

But fierce storms soon hit the ship.

Can you make the ship go any faster?

I'm working the engines as they have never been worked before.

If I fail, I will never return to New York. I would rather go in dead and successful than alive and behind time.

On January 21, the *Oceanic* sailed into San Francisco Bay. It was a day later than the chief engineer's prediction, but Nellie was still ahead of schedule. Yet her plan to head east to New Jersey by train hit a snag.

A huge blizzard has shut down the trains crossing California's mountains.

I've traveled so far. Is this how my trip will end?

Luckily, the *World* stepped in. The paper arranged Nellie's first and only special transportation—a train that took her south of the snow and then on to New Jersey. Along the way, Nellie was met by cheering crowds.

Hurrah for Nellie Bly!

Nellie! You should run for governor!

Nellie reached her final destination of Jersey City, New Jersey, on January 25, 1890, at 3:51 p.m. Her journey around the world had lasted 72 days, 6 hours, and 11 minutes. She was two days ahead of schedule.

Ah, I'm finally home!

Chapter 4 Nellie's Legacy

Nellie's trip around the world made her a national celebrity. Women began wearing outfits based on the clothes she wore on her trip.

Her picture was used to sell all sorts of products from soap to cigars. A racehorse was named after her. There was even a Nellie Bly board game.

Oh no, I've just had to go back three days!

Thanks to Nellie's daring trip, the *World* sold more papers than ever before. The paper even sold an "authorized biography" of Nellie.

NELLIE BLY

Nellie expected a raise or a bonus for her hard work, but she didn't receive either.

So she resigned from the paper and went on a lecture tour. She also wrote *Nellie Bly's Book: Around the World in Seventy-Two Days,* which became a bestseller.

Through sheer hard work and perseverance, Nellie Bly made herself into the most famous newspaper reporter in the United States.

At a time when women weren't allowed to vote, few had careers, and even fewer traveled alone (or with a monkey), Nellie set an example. Her adventures showed women what they could do if they only dared.

Nothing is impossible if one applies a certain amount of energy in the right direction.

MORE ABOUT NELLIE BLY

- Nellie Bly is the most famous of the girl stunt reporters of her time. She went undercover as a factory worker to show the poor pay and treatment of young girls working at a paper-box factory. She also almost bought a baby to expose the illegal selling of infants. But not all her reporting was grim. She also wrote about learning to fence and being in a chorus line. Nellie even spent a night in a haunted house waiting for a ghost!

- One of Nellie's most famous pieces of reporting was done undercover as a mentally ill patient at the Women's Asylum on Blackwell's Island. Her exposé of the asylum's horrific conditions caused a sensation and helped bring more funding and improvements in patient care. Nellie wrote a best-selling book called *Ten Days in a Mad-House* about her experience.

- Elizabeth Bisland, Nellie Bly's competitor, also beat Phileas Fogg's fictional record. But it took her 76 days to go around the world. Nellie beat her by four days.

- When Nellie was 31, she left reporting to marry Robert Seaman, a millionaire businessman in his 70s. Nellie immersed herself in his business and eventually became president of Seaman's Iron Clad Manufacturing Company. The company turned sheet metal into milk cans, wash tubs, boilers, and more. Nellie became an inventor too. She held patents for a new kind of milk can and a stacking garbage can.

- Upon Seaman's death, Nellie instituted ahead-of-their-times worker-friendly policies including weekly wages. She built an on-site library and gymnasium for her employees to use, and even a small hospital. Unfortunately, Nellie lost her company and her money to dishonest accountants and employees.

- In her later years, Nellie returned to reporting. She became a frontline World War I correspondent in Austria and then an advice columnist helping women and children in need.

- Nellie never stopped working. Her last newspaper column was published a few weeks before her death from pneumonia on January 27, 1922. She was 57 years old.

- For all Nellie's groundbreaking work, it's important to remember that she shared many of the prejudices people held in the 1800s. They are revealed in her book about her journey, *Around the World in Seventy-Two Days*. Nellie sometimes uses language, descriptions, and stereotypes that were wrong back then and are still wrong today.

GLOSSARY

asylum (uh-SYE-luhm)—a hospital for people who are mentally ill

celebrity (sell-EH-bruh-tee)—a famous person or animal

correspondent (kor-uh-SPON-duhnt)—someone who reports for television, radio, or newspapers

destination (des-tuh-NAY-shuhn)—the place to which one is traveling

editor (ED-uh-tur)—the person in charge of a newspaper or a magazine

exposé (ek-spoh-ZAY)—a report of facts that reveals something shocking or scandalous

passport (PASS-port)—an official booklet that proves that a person is a citizen of a certain country; passports allow people to travel to foreign countries

pneumonia (noo-MOH-nyuh)—a serious disease that causes the lungs to become inflamed and filled with a thick fluid that makes breathing difficult

prejudices (PREJ-uh-diss-ess)—beliefs that are not based on facts or knowledge

rickshaw (RIK-shaw)—a small carriage that is usually pulled by a person

telegraph (TEL-uh-graf)—a machine that uses electronic signals to send messages over long distances

transcontinental (transs-kon-tuh-NEN-tuhl)—crossing a continent

translator (TRANSS-lay-tur)—a person who changes words from one language to another

READ MORE

Gurevich, Margaret. *Who Was Nellie Bly?* New York: Penguin Workshop, 2020.

Knudsen, Michelle. *She Persisted: Nellie Bly.* New York: Philomel, 2021.

Leavitt, Amie Jane. *Nellie Bly.* Kennet Square, PA: Purple Toad Publishing, 2018.

INTERNET SITES

American Experience: Around the World in 72 Days
pbs.org/wgbh/americanexperience/films/world

Biography: Nellie Bly
biography.com/activist/nellie-bly

Senator John Heinz History Center: Nellie Bly: Around the World
heinzhistorycenter.org/learn/women-forging-the-way/nellie-bly-around-the-world

ABOUT THE AUTHOR

Agnieszka Biskup is a writer and editor who lives in Chicago. She was an editor at the *Boston Globe* newspaper and studied science journalism at MIT. Agnieszka was also the managing editor of the children's magazine *Muse*. She has written many children's books, as well as articles for newspapers, magazines, and the web. Her books have won many awards, including an American Institute of Physics Science Writing Award, where instead of a trophy, she got a chair. (Yes, the kind you sit in. It is very nice.)

photo by Agnieszka Biskup

ABOUT THE ILLUSTRATOR

Natalia Galindo is an illustrator whose love for pencils, brushes, and colors as a child blossomed into a passion for art. After high school, she focused all of her time and energy into developing her skills as an illustrator and earned a position at Red Wolf Studios. While with Red Wolf, she has created covers, developed interior art, and facilitated coloration on numerous projects for dozens of independent publishers.

photo by Natalia Galindo